NATIONAL
GEOGRAPHIC
KiDS

125 Cute Animals

125
Cute Animals

MEET THE CUTEST CRITTERS ON THE PLANET, INCLUDING ANIMALS YOU NEVER KNEW EXISTED, AND SOME SO UGLY, THEY'RE CUTE.

NATIONAL GEOGRAPHIC KiDS

WASHINGTON, D.C.

Contents

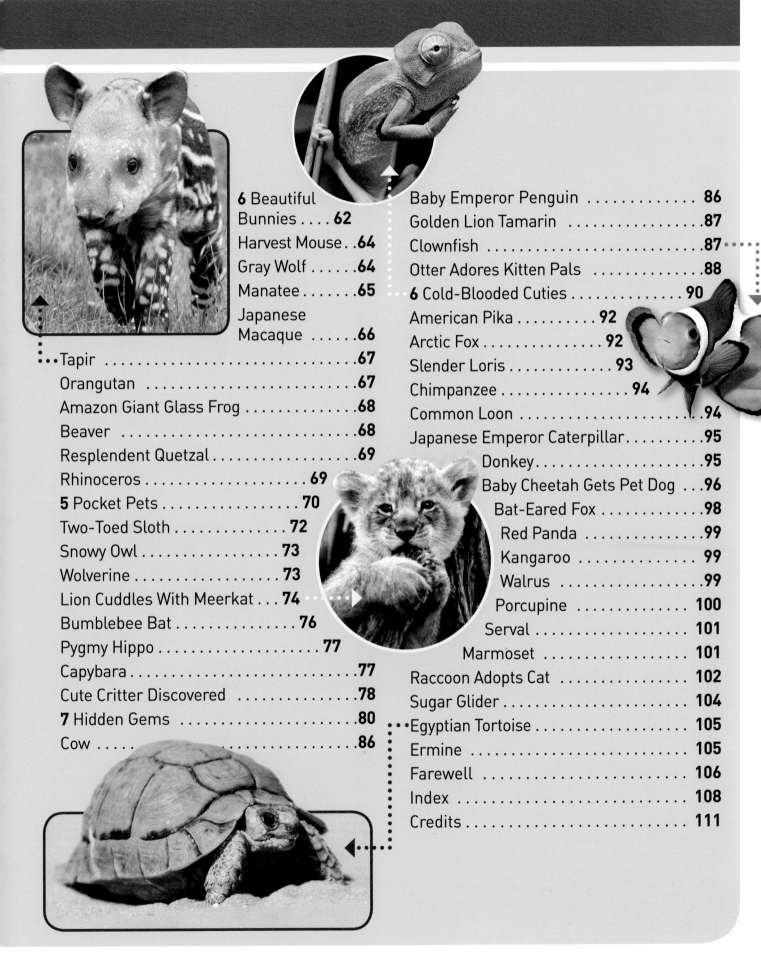

Introduction

WELCOME to the heartwarming world of cute animals.

Paw through these pages and find 125 of National Geographic Kids' favorite cuties and more! Meet Bengal tiger cubs and a baby beluga whale. Check out cuteness from pea puffer fish to ponies.

These adorable stories are not only fun to read, they may also push the limits of how cute you thought animals could be! So let the ooohs and awwws begin, and join this amazing parade of cute animals.

WELSH MOUNTAIN PONIES

RACCOON

PEA PUFFER FISH

BELUGA WHALES

BENGAL TIGER

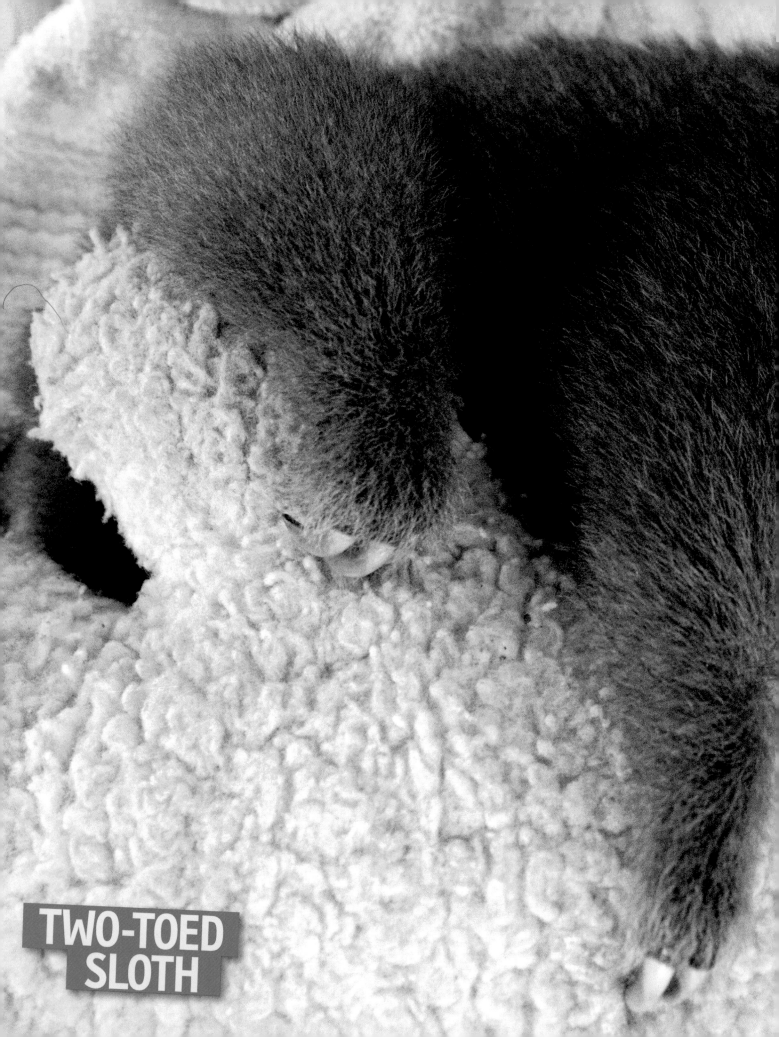

TWO-TOED SLOTH

The platypus is one of only five mammals known to lay eggs. The other four are all species of echidna.

PLATYPUS

Looking like a mix of duck, beaver, and otter, this three-pound (1.5-kg) Aussie has sharp, venomous stingers on its rear feet. The graceful platypus hunts underwater, paddling its webbed feet along a water-bottom buffet of insects, shellfish, and worms. The toothless mammal also scoops up pebbles to help him chew. With its cheek pouches full, the platypus swims to the surface of the water, where he makes a mouthwatering mash.

The ruby-throated hummingbird glistens and sparkles as it beats its wings about 50 times per second. The delicate bird hovers to feed on flowers, nectar, and sap. These little beauties breed in the eastern United States. But when winter comes, they head for warmer weather in Mexico and Central America. To get there, they hop a nonstop flight all the way across the Gulf of Mexico. In spring, they return home.

RUBY-THROATED HUMMINGBIRD

ALPACA

A relative of the camel, these four-legged fur balls are known for their luxurious, warm fleece. It grows in 22 colors, from white to brown to silver and black. The alpaca's fantastic fleece was once reserved for Inca royalty. But you don't have to go to the mountains of South America to meet a friendly, fuzzy alpaca. Today, they can be found on farms all over the world.

Instead of hooves, alpacas have soft padded feet, each with two toes.

CHIPMUNK

This North American rodent stays alert while it fills its cheek pouches with everything from seeds and nuts to worms and bird eggs. If danger comes along, it calls loudly to warn other chipmunks. Hey, dude! Don't talk with your mouth full!

A newborn chipmunk weighs less than a chocolate kiss.

I'D STICK MY NECK OUT FOR THIS GUY ANYTIME!

Turn that frown upside down, baby ostrich! This bouncing baby will grow to a monstrous size and will run fast on superlong, strong legs. His huge size makes sense—the egg he hatched from weighed as much as two dozen chicken eggs! As an adult, he'll be able to run about as fast as a race horse and kill a lion with powerful kicks. Pow!

BABY OSTRICH LOVES TOY

Pembrokeshire, Wales

Birds aren't known for loving toys, but Madoc the baby ostrich can't get enough of his stuffed animal. Madoc lives with his fluff-filled "friend" at the Folly Farm Adventure Park and Zoo. After Madoc was abandoned by his mom, caretakers gave the newborn the toy to keep him company. "The stuffed animal is like a security blanket," zoo manager Tim Morphew says. "It makes Madoc feel safe."

The ostrich eats with the toy next to him and sleeps squatting at its feet. Sometimes Madoc gently nuzzles his bestie with his beak. If someone moves the toy, Madoc waddles over to join it. "Baby birds learn what kind of creatures they are by watching family members," says Stephen Kress of the National Audubon Society. "Madoc's toy look-alike is showing him he's an ostrich." The little guy soon may outgrow the need for a stuffed buddy. But for now, these birds of a different feather still flock together.

To hide from a lion, an ostrich might lie down and press its neck to the ground.

The wings on these ostrich babies won't help them fly when they grow up but will make great rudders for fast turns.

7 DARLING

ENGLISH BULLDOG
With their heavy front ends, bulldog puppies snuggle better than they swim.

AFFEN-PINSCHER
In German, the name of this peppy little pup means "monkey terrier."

GOLDEN RETRIEVER
Often referred to as "goldens," these sweet pups are so smart that they're frequently used as guide dogs for the blind.

DOGS

PUG
Pugs have been people's pets since at least A.D. 950!

RESCUE DOG
Millions of rescued dogs wait in shelters for their forever homes every year.

GERMAN SHEPHERD
A German shepherd's ears usually stand up straight by the time it's two years old.

GRAND BASSET GRIFFON VENDÉEN
This fluffy French breed is known for its quick feet, courageous heart, and good manners.

BROWN BEAR

In the fall, these brown bear cubs will each start packing on about three pounds (1.5 kg) a day to prepare for their deep winter sleep. Those pounds of fat are what the bears will live on while snoozing all winter. Luckily, Mom is an expert at sniffing out a meal in their northwestern United States habitat and can detect food from 18 miles (29 km) away.

A brown bear, like a grizzly, can live to be 25 years old in the wild.

For safety in numbers, family groups of zebras sometimes join up to create one massive herd.

PLAINS ZEBRA

Scientists can't say for sure why these wild African equines have stripes, but it's likely a means of camouflage. A new theory suggests the stripes might even help zebras repel biting insects. Other theories say that stripes provide natural sunscreen and a way for zebras to identify each other. Like their wild horse cousins, plains zebras live in herds made up of a lead male, a group of females, and their babies, like this frisky little cutie.

A bush baby gets around on four legs but can also hop like a kangaroo.

LESSER BUSH BABY

These teeny primates make lots of noise. Their screechy cries, peeps, croaks, and clucks can be heard all night in the African bush. If they spot a predator like a snake or an owl, they whistle in warning. Groups of bush babies live together in trees, venturing down to the ground at night to prey on beetles, grasshoppers, and small reptiles. During the day, bush babies congregate in trees to catch some z's.

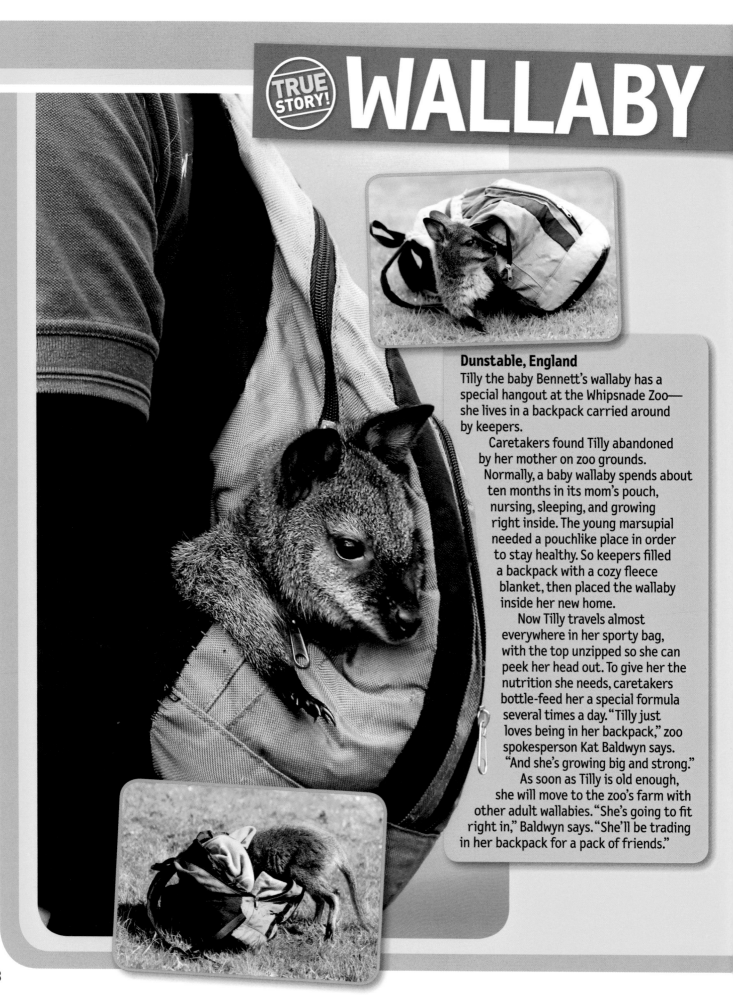

Dunstable, England

Tilly the baby Bennett's wallaby has a special hangout at the Whipsnade Zoo—she lives in a backpack carried around by keepers.

Caretakers found Tilly abandoned by her mother on zoo grounds. Normally, a baby wallaby spends about ten months in its mom's pouch, nursing, sleeping, and growing right inside. The young marsupial needed a pouchlike place in order to stay healthy. So keepers filled a backpack with a cozy fleece blanket, then placed the wallaby inside her new home.

Now Tilly travels almost everywhere in her sporty bag, with the top unzipped so she can peek her head out. To give her the nutrition she needs, caretakers bottle-feed her a special formula several times a day. "Tilly just loves being in her backpack," zoo spokesperson Kat Baldwyn says. "And she's growing big and strong."

As soon as Tilly is old enough, she will move to the zoo's farm with other adult wallabies. "She's going to fit right in," Baldwyn says. "She'll be trading in her backpack for a pack of friends."

HANGS OUT
IN BACKPACK

Uh-oh ... better watch out or this cute wallaby might mob you! But that just means you'll be meeting its family. Wallabies and their young live in groups called mobs. These cute-looking creatures are not pushovers, though. Males will box each other over a mate. Plus, they can survive for long periods without water in the dry Australian climate, gathering nutrients and moisture from plants.

Like its kangaroo cousins, a young wallaby is called a joey.

Boing! A juvenile wallaby might jump back into its mother's pouch if startled or scared.

SO UGLY,

LANGUR

This baby monkey looks like a weird elf now, but soon the little one will grow long gray or gold hair. In one city in India, 2,100 of these revered wild monkeys are regularly fed and have buffet privileges at local gardens and picnics.

Langur monkeys in India often share their steamy rain forest habitat with Bengal tigers and Asian elephants, but they can live in other places, too, including cities!

THEY'RE CUTE

The star of the show, this nearly blind mole's nose is made up of 22 soft tentacles that help it find food.

STAR-NOSED MOLE

This über-predator lives underground to be near the worms and insects it loves to eat. Forget about eyes, all this rodent needs to survive is its sense of touch. It presses its pink feelers into the dirt to detect prey. When it finds something good, the mole scarfs down a luscious meal lickety-split.

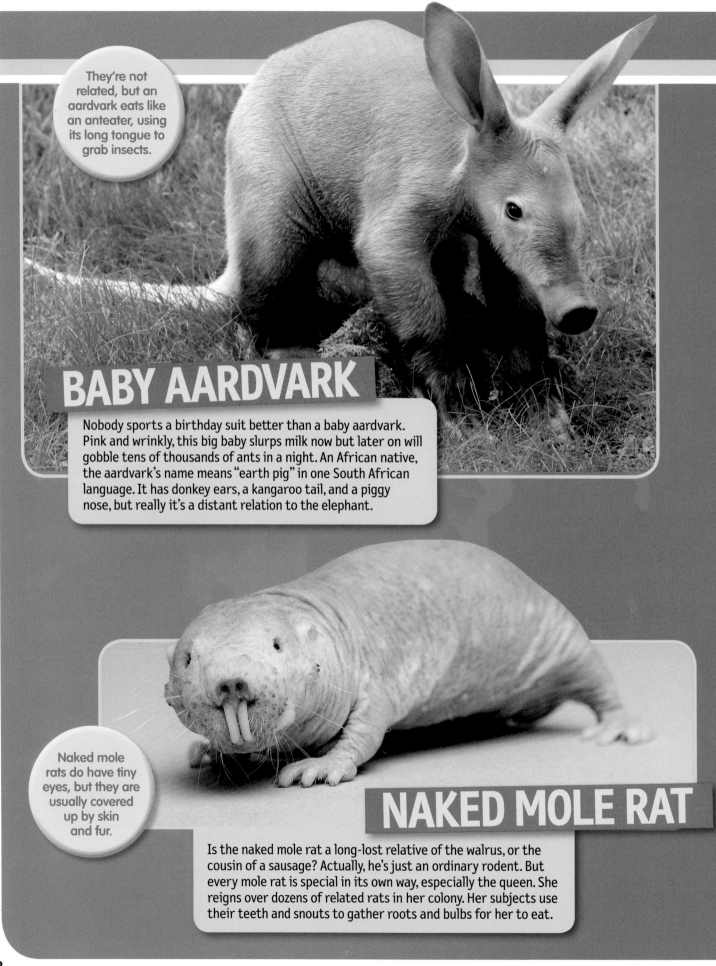

They're not related, but an aardvark eats like an anteater, using its long tongue to grab insects.

BABY AARDVARK

Nobody sports a birthday suit better than a baby aardvark. Pink and wrinkly, this big baby slurps milk now but later on will gobble tens of thousands of ants in a night. An African native, the aardvark's name means "earth pig" in one South African language. It has donkey ears, a kangaroo tail, and a piggy nose, but really it's a distant relation to the elephant.

Naked mole rats do have tiny eyes, but they are usually covered up by skin and fur.

NAKED MOLE RAT

Is the naked mole rat a long-lost relative of the walrus, or the cousin of a sausage? Actually, he's just an ordinary rodent. But every mole rat is special in its own way, especially the queen. She reigns over dozens of related rats in her colony. Her subjects use their teeth and snouts to gather roots and bulbs for her to eat.

Not the most down-to-earth animal you've ever met, the aye-aye spends most of his life up in the trees.

AYE-AYE

Did you know we humans are related to the adorable aye-aye? But, as you can see, these pie-eyed primates don't look much like us. They have bushy tails bigger than their bodies, huge ears, and pointed claws. Aye-ayes live in the rain forests of Madagascar, where their favorite nighttime activities are dangling from branches and digging for irresistible insect larvae. When morning comes, the aye-aye curls up in a ball and sleeps all day.

JUMPING SPIDER

This harmless hurdler is small enough to perch on your fingernail. Blink and you might miss it, but it certainly won't miss you. The jumping spider has not two, not four, but eight eyes that jut out from its fierce little face. If you can get close enough, you'll be surprised to see the spider grooming much like a cat would—wiping its eyes and cleaning its claws. But be quick! Before you know it, the spider will hop, hop away.

Jumping spiders pounce on their prey instead of relying on silk webs to capture food.

A baby parrot hatches out of its shell naked and blind.

BABY PARROT

Helpless and featherless, a baby parrot will soon grow up to be a bold, beautiful bird. But for now, it's growing feathers one day at a time. Parrots start "fledging," or practicing their flying skills, when three to four months old. They'll pick a favorite perch and learn important lessons about landing—wings down, feet out—with lots of trial and error.

PINK FAIRY ARMADILLO

With her pink plates of armor and fluffy white fur, the petite pink fairy armadillo could pass for a fashion accessory—or maybe a giant piece of sushi! Born with custom claws specially designed for digging, it can bury itself superfast if it's in danger.

The pink fairy armadillo lives wild in central Argentina's dry grasslands.

OPOSSUM

Hang in there, buddy! Opossums have some cool secret powers, including expert climbing skills. They're also immune to rattlesnake venom. Plus, opossums have 50 teeth, more than any other North American land mammal.

Not a picky eater, an opossum will eat almost any kind of food it finds.

25

The name "jaguar" comes from the Native American word *yaguar*, which means "he who kills with one leap."

BLACK JAGUAR

This big cat may be called "panther" sometimes, but really he's a jaguar from South America—the biggest of the big cats in that area of the world. Jaguars of any color—black or the traditional orange coat with black spots (called rosettes)—are threatened by people hunting the animals—including cubs like this one—for their beautiful coat.

RED-EYED TREE FROG

These red eyes aren't just for show. If a hungry snake approaches a sleeping frog, it can flash the bright red color and hopefully startle the predator. Then the frog, which lives in rain forests of southern Mexico and Central and South America, can hop away.

A red-eyed tree frog will eat any food that fits in its mouth.

WILD BOAR

You wouldn't want to mess with these little guys after they're about a year old. That's when wild boars start growing permanent tusks. They use them to scratch trees (wild boar code for "This is *my* space.") and defend themselves from predators or other boars. Like their pig cousins, wild boars are thought to be supersmart and communicate with a complex set of grunts and squeals.

A "sounder" is a gathering of 50 to 100 wild boars.

BOBCAT

These bobcats may have some of the finest fur coats in the animal world, but they are not for show. The spotted fur helps North America's most common wild cat blend in with many habitats, from swamps to deserts to mountains. Those ear tufts? Bobcats may twitch them to communicate with other bobcats.

DUCKLING

A duckling is a true copycat. When ducklings hatch, they mimic their mother's every action, from eating to swimming to waddling. (The mimicking behavior is called imprinting.) But they don't copy Mom's look. Ducklings won't replace their yellow fuzz with adult feathers until they're about two months old.

After hatching, a duckling will follow the first "mother" it sees.

Squirrels run fast— up to 20 miles an hour (32 km/h).

GRAY SQUIRREL

These fuzzy rodents help plant oak trees all over the world by burying their acorns and then forgetting where they are. It's called "scatter hoarding." But nuts aren't the only thing squirrels like to eat. They nibble on berries, roots, and flowers, holding their meal with their front feet. There are nearly 200 squirrel species living almost all over the world; Australia is the only place in the world (besides Antarctica and Greenland) where furry-tailed, nut-obsessed squirrels *don't* live.

Kinkajous swivel their hind feet front or back, depending on which way they want to run along a branch.

KINKAJOU

The contagiously cute kinkajou looks like a little monkey but is actually related to the raccoon. These little mammals love to slurp honey from beehives with their long, skinny tongues. That's what earned them the nickname "honey bear." But a kinkajou's sweet tooth doesn't stop there. It also loves fruit and flower nectar. What a sweetie!

I SHOULD'VE CHECKED THE FORECAST THIS MORNING.

Scientists say lemurs may have floated to their island home of Madagascar centuries ago on vegetation "rafts."

West Midlands, England

Yoda the black-and-white ruffed lemur didn't let a little rain spoil his day. Instead, the brainy critter scored himself an umbrella!

The primate had been roaming around his open area at the Dudley Zoological Gardens one drizzly morning when he saw a woman with an open umbrella. Getting close, he tapped on her leg. The startled visitor dropped her rain gear, and Yoda immediately plucked it off the ground. He twirled it around by the handle and reached up to touch the umbrella's smooth fabric canopy. Then, holding the umbrella over his head, the lemur dashed away. Yoda dropped the rain protection only when a gust of wind nearly knocked him down.

Although Yoda avoided getting soaked by snagging the gear, staying dry may not have been his main goal. "Lemurs don't mind getting a little wet," zoo senior curator Derek Grove says. In fact, he may have been feeling curious—and playful. Says Grove, "Rain or shine, Yoda likes to have fun."

UMBRELLA

A ring-tailed lemur can live up to 18 years in the wild.

With more than 100 known species of lemurs, the ring-tailed lemur has many cousins.

These spunky primates live in the wild on the African island of Madagascar. Like little striped acrobats, lemurs swing from tree limb to tree limb, grabbing and eating leaves, flowers, tree bark, and fruit. If it's mating time, a male lemur will try to scare off other males with a smelly warning. He uses the scent glands on his wrist and shoulders to douse his tail in stinky secretions; then he waves it around, trying to outstink other males. Can you imagine if humans did something like that?

When it moves around, the sifaka lemur throws its arms in the air and does a little hop, skip, and a jump.

After it climbs out of the water, a polar bear shakes like a dog to dry its coat.

POLAR BEAR

This cute polar bear will grow up to be a fierce predator built for surviving in the bitter cold. In winter, a polar bear's body can have up to four inches (10 cm) of blubber under two layers of fur to keep it warm. These carnivores of the Arctic region can pick up a seal's scent 20 miles (32 km) away.

KOALA

An Australian cutie like this koala will never need to go to day care with Mom around! A young koala lives in its mother's pouch for about six months—easy to do when you're born the size of a jelly bean. And don't call them bears. Koalas are actually marsupials, pouched animals like kangaroos.

MOUNTAIN GORILLA

This gorilla may be off to a playdate. Young mountain gorillas spend their days having fun: climbing trees, chasing each other, and swinging from branches. But it's not all fun and games for this gentle species. The mountain gorilla is one of the most endangered species, with only 700 left in the wild in Africa.

7 PURR-FECT

EGYPTIAN MAU
This super-sleepy Egyptian mau kitten has spots that resemble the spots on a cheetah. This breed can be trained to fetch like a dog.

MAINE COON
One of the oldest American breeds of cat, this little kitten can grow to be more than 20 pounds (9 kg) and has tufts of fur on his ears and his feet.

NORWEGIAN FOREST CAT
Nicknamed "wegies," these super-fluffy cats from Norway are thought to be extremely intelligent.

CATS

RESCUE KITTEN
Some of the cutest kitties in the world are waiting to be adopted at animal shelters.

SINGAPURA
Small but strong, the Singapura has a reputation for taking the lead in training humans—and any dog it meets.

PIXIEBOB
Bred to look like a bobcat, these rugged kitties love to play in the water.

BIRMAN
This silky-coated, blue-eyed feline comes in colors called blue, chocolate, lilac, and parti-color.

Endangered Amur leopards live alongside Siberian tigers in the snowy Russian Far East.

LEOPARD

Leopards, like this cub, love hanging out in trees. Adults sometimes hunt from up in trees, where their spots help them blend in with the leafy branches. The big cats pounce from above, without warning. These beautiful spotted hunters live in parts of Africa and Asia. The leopard's dark spots are called rosettes, because they are shaped like a rose. These spots also help the leopard blend in with tall grass.

WHITE TERN

White tern chicks get a surprise when they hatch. These tropical birds find themselves precariously perched on a tree branch or ledge instead of tucked into a nest. Why? That's where their mothers have balanced the eggs. Luckily, baby terns have strong feet to keep a grip on things.

The white tern's angel-like wings appear almost translucent in the light.

COYOTE

A howl from a coyote pup may sound more like a high-pitched squeal, but hearing howls from the entire pack can sound a little spooky. Don't worry—they're mostly just checking on their pals. Coyotes use certain types of vocalizations to communicate in different situations. One type of howl rallies the pack for a hunt. Another helps a lost coyote find his friends. No wonder coyotes are often portrayed as extremely brainy in Native American folklore.

Coyotes are strong swimmers.

Pigs are highly trainable animals, and some people keep them as pets, like dogs.

PIG

This little guy may not look so cute once he finds himself a mudhole. Pigs love to wallow in mud—it's like natural air-conditioning. They can't sweat, so taking a dip in a mud puddle helps them keep cool. The mud also acts as a natural sunscreen.

TRUE STORY!

MY BEST BUDDY IS A BIG SOFTIE!

All bears today are descendants of an animal that existed 30 million years ago and looked like a cross between a raccoon and a dog.

CUB CUDDLES

Portland, Oregon, U.S.A.

Aldo the black bear cub is definitely cute. But when he was playing with his plush beaver toy, he was *ultra*-adorable. "He'd fuss if you ever moved it," says Oregon Zoo keeper Michelle Schireman, who used to care for Aldo.

The orphaned cub was brought to the zoo after being found alone in the woods. Soon the exhausted and hungry bear grew healthy—and very energetic. "He played with every object in sight, including my shoes," Schireman says. "So we decided to get him his very own toy." The cub immediately bonded with his new bestie. He loved belly flopping onto the stuffed animal and play-wrestling with it. He'd drag the soft toy around with him and nuzzle it before sleeping.

"Like people, bear cubs can feel comforted by warm and fuzzy things, including stuffed animals," says Carmen Murach, an animal curator at the Northeastern Wisconsin Zoo, where Aldo eventually moved. Now older, Aldo has outgrown his need for a stuffed animal. But he's found another toy to play with: a plastic penguin!

Bear-y cute! These cautious creatures weigh as little as a hockey puck when they're born and even purr as they nurse from their mother. After they stop drinking milk, North America's black bears munch on almost anything—insects, nuts and berries, and even grass.

GIRAFFE

Like striped tigers and zebras, this baby giraffe's spotty coat has a unique pattern. At birth, a giraffe can weigh 150 pounds (68 kg) and stand 6 feet (2 m) tall. As adults, these gentle giants can weigh as much as 2,800 pounds (1,270 kg) and stand 19 feet (6 m) tall. A giraffe uses its height to its advantage—eating tasty buds at the tops of trees that no antelope could reach and watching out for sneaky predators—like lions—that share its African home.

In South Africa, a pet giraffe named Fenne liked to hang out inside her rescuer's house.

BLACK-FOOTED FERRET

Black-footed ferrets are all business. That is, a group of ferrets in the wild is called a "business." These masked bandits—also known as American polecats—have long, slender bodies that make it easy for them to slink through prairie-dog villages, one of their favorite "restaurants." These ferrets are endangered in the wild and are a different species from the ferret you might have as a pet at home. Domesticated ferrets are relations of the European polecat and are highly trainable. Some owners even take them around for walks on a leash—like a dog!

Every year, the British Ferret Club in England hosts competitions for domesticated show ferrets.

This snappy baby alligator might grow and lose 3,000 teeth during its lifetime.

AMERICAN ALLIGATOR

It may take a while before this baby alligator can spell his family's scientific name: Alligatoridae. Meanwhile, these yellow-striped babies (a group is called a pod) are busy growing. Born at 6 to 8 inches (15 to 20 cm) long, a male can grow to be about 11 feet (3.5 m) long and can weigh half a ton (453 kg). In the wild, these rugged reptiles can be found in the swamps, lakes, and marshes of the American South.

Snow leopards' favorite foods are blue sheep, hares, wild goats, and birds.

SNOW LEOPARD

Nice fur coat! Snow leopards live in some of the coldest parts of Asia, where they need the fluffiest, fuzziest fur to keep warm. These rare cats have large, fur-covered paws that act like snowshoes so they don't sink into deep snow. Snow leopards also beat the chill by sleeping with their superthick tails wrapped around them like a furry scarf.

Killer whales are referred to as "orcas" because of their scientific name, *Orcinus orca*.

KILLER WHALE

Even though it is called a killer whale, the orca is actually the largest species in the dolphin family. A bouncing baby orca calf weighs about 400 pounds (180 kg) at birth and stays with its mother for about two years. Orcas live in social groups called pods. A pod functions like a pack of wolves—with the animals living together, caring for each other, and hunting together.

AIN'T LOVE GRAND!

GENTOO PENGUIN

These recently hatched baby birds look ready to explore their home in the Antarctic area, but they'll actually stay with Mom in the nest for up to a month. Gentoo penguins build nests of pebbles and moss. Some gentoos even bring their partners pebbles as gifts.

A gentoo penguin might dive into the water 450 times a day, foraging for food.

7 PRETTY HORSES

APPALOOSA
Spotted horses like this leopard-spotted Appaloosa have been seen in prehistoric cave drawings.

CHINCOTEAGUE PONY
Sturdy and spirited, many Chincoteague ponies are descended from domestic horses but now live wild on the 37-mile (60-km)-long barrier island called Assateague Island in the mid-Atlantic United States.

WELSH MOUNTAIN PONY
For generations, bands of these cute-as-a-button yet semiwild ponies survived long, cold, wet winters in the rough hills and valleys of Wales.

CLYDESDALE
Have you ever heard of a horse with feathers? This beautiful Clydesdale has feathered hooves—luxurious hair that protects the horse's feet.

RESCUE HORSE
Rescued horses come in all ages, breeds, shapes, sizes, and colors.

MINIATURE HORSE
Imported from Europe in the early 1900s, miniature horses pulled carts in and out of cramped coal-mine tunnels.

ANDALUSIAN
The Andalusian breed of horse originated in Spain and Portugal and is known for its power and beauty.

ECHIDNA

If you thought a puggle was a cross between a pug and a beagle, think again. The eastern long-beaked echidna baby is also called a puggle. A walking, sniffing ball of spines, the puggle's egg-laying mother is on a mission to find insects. She uses her strong sense of smell and her long beak to find a colony of ants under the ground. Then, slurp! She uses her long, sticky tongue to snatch the insects. How's that for a drive-through meal?

Eastern long-beaked echidnas have rows of sharp spine-like structures on their tongue to help them grab delicious earthworms.

LOGGERHEAD SEA TURTLE

This baby loggerhead is a true survivor. First it broke out of an egg the size of a Ping-Pong ball. Then it dug itself out from a buried nest on a beach. After that, it scurried from the beach to the ocean, dodging predators such as crabs and herons. (You try doing that with flippers instead of feet!) And still no sign of relief—once it reached the surf, the turtle swam for 24 hours straight to move farther out to sea, where it will have an easier time avoiding predators.

ATLANTIC PUFFIN

A baby puffin is called a puffling.

In the air, an Atlantic puffin flaps its wings as many as 400 times a minute and can speed along at a whopping 55 miles an hour (88 km/h), as fast as a car on a highway. But these seaworthy birds spend more time in the water than in the air. Atlantic puffins "fly" in the water, using their wings as paddles. This way, they stay close to their favorite foods. Puffins dive as deep as 200 feet (61 m) to snatch small fish.

WHITE-TAILED DEER

Deer often sniff to identify each other or just to say hello. These fawns are having a playdate while their mothers forage for food nearby. Their spotted coats help them blend into their forest home. After three or four months, the spots fade and the brown coat grows thick for the winter.

White-tailed deer usually browse for food at dawn.

HOO-HOO-WHO'S NUMBER ONE?

In the wild, burrowing owls nest in homes dug out by prairie dogs, squirrels, and armadillos. They line their nests with cow or horse poop to attract insects that they can eat while still in their nests (talk about breakfast in bed!). But when it's time for lunch, burrowing owls hunt on the ground or from strategically placed perches, racing to snatch up tasty grasshoppers, beetles, mice, and small reptiles.

Burrowing owls can often be seen in wide-open spaces that are covered with short grass, such as golf courses and airports.

TRUE STORY! OWL RUNS RACES

London, England

Watching Bob the burrowing owl get a workout is a real hoot—this bird *enjoys* running. "His long legs are like a blur when he's on the move," says animal trainer Jim Mackie of the ZSL London Zoo, where Bob lives.

Most owl species hunt prey from the air while flying. But burrowing owls such as Bob stay grounded as they search for grub. So these birds are used to scuttling around on their legs. Bob is so fast that his keepers built him a three-foot (1-m)-long track complete with a finish line so he could practice sprinting. Placing his wings at his side and leaning his body forward, the feathered runner will charge from one end of the track to the other. To refuel after a jog, Bob chomps fat mealworms.

The owl has even competed in "races." During a zoo event, various animals sprinted the same distance separately, and then keepers compared their running times. Although Bob wasn't quite as fast as one speedy armadillo, the bird wasn't fazed. "He's more interested in his post-run snack than in winning," Mackie says. Bob must be a good sport!

Burrowing owls communicate with each other by clucking or chattering.

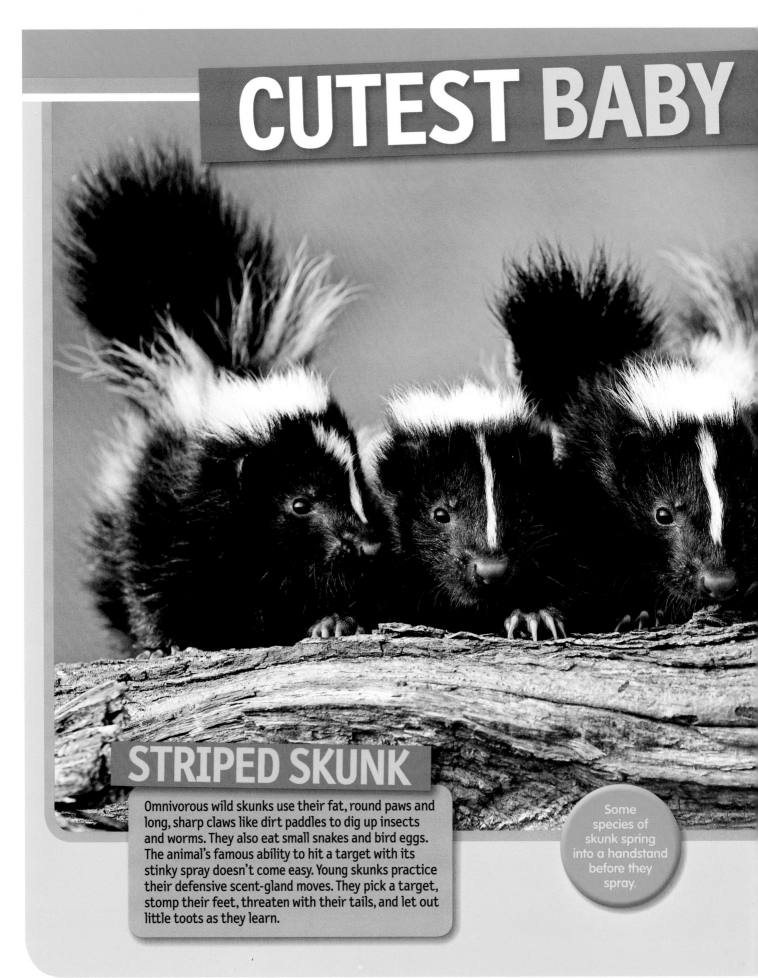

CUTEST BABY

STRIPED SKUNK

Omnivorous wild skunks use their fat, round paws and long, sharp claws like dirt paddles to dig up insects and worms. They also eat small snakes and bird eggs. The animal's famous ability to hit a target with its stinky spray doesn't come easy. Young skunks practice their defensive scent-gland moves. They pick a target, stomp their feet, threaten with their tails, and let out little toots as they learn.

Some species of skunk spring into a handstand before they spray.

ANIMALS

HARP SEAL

If you're ever in snowy Arctic Russia or Canada, be sure to walk carefully—you might mistake a newborn harp seal for a pile of snow! At about two weeks old, the pup sheds its furry white coat for one that's gray and smooth, perfect for skimming through the ocean to hunt for small fish. While hunting, harp seals can hold their breath for up to 20 minutes while they dive to depths of 800 feet (244 m) or more. That's as deep as the Eiffel Tower is tall!

Baby seals are born on floating ice.

CUTEST BABY ANIMALS

In the wild, female elephants—mothers, sisters, aunts, daughters, and cousins—often live together their entire lives.

AFRICAN ELEPHANT

Get out of these elephants' way! African elephants can weigh some 200 pounds (91 kg) at birth; by adulthood, they can top the scales at more than 7 tons (6,350 kg). The world's largest land mammal also has a big appetite, eating more than 300 pounds (136 kg) of grass, fruit, and leaves a day.

Elephants use their trunks to hug each other.

SAND CAT

This rare, fluffy-faced feline lives wild in northern Africa and southwest and central Asia. Its soft, sandy-colored coat provides camouflage and keeps it warm at night and cool during the day. It has a great sense of hearing that helps it detect the scurrying feet of the desert delicacies it loves to eat, including gerbils, reptiles, and insects. It also eats snakes, bopping them on the head and biting them on the neck before devouring them.

Sand cats have furry feet that keep them from sinking in the sand.

BELUGA WHALE

This marine baby snuggles with its mom. The bouncing baby beluga may have weighed a whopping 175 pounds (80 kg) at birth. These chatty whales make so many squeaks, squawks, shrieks, clicks, screeches, and snorts that scientists call them "sea canaries." They bounce the sounds off the objects in Arctic waters to create a "picture" of what they hear.

Baby beluga whales are born gray or even brown and slowly whiten over five years.

A saw-whet owl's right ear is higher on its head than the left ear, which improves its hearing and helps it hunt.

SAW-WHET OWL

Hear the sound of a saw being sharpened on a stone? If you're in the woods of the western and northeastern United States or Canada, it could be the alarm call of a saw-whet owl. This bird may be small, but the seven- to eight-inch (17- to 20-cm)-tall owl is a swift and fierce night hunter, swooping down on unsuspecting mice, chipmunks, and squirrels under the cover of darkness.

BENGAL TIGER

This tiger cub isn't likely to get lost. Like all tigers, it has white markings on the backs of its ears that help the mother tiger keep an eye on her cubs. Adult Bengal tigers are sneaky hunters. Their stripes help them hide in tall grass where they live in India so they can sneak up on prey.

Bengal tigers in India share their hot habitat with clouded leopards and Asian elephants.

MOUNTAIN GOAT

Cute? No kidding! Mountain goat babies, or kids, live with their moms, called nannies, in herds of 10 to 20 individuals in parts of North America. All mountain goats grow white beards and can climb better than most other animals. In order to survive, the cuddly kids must climb the scraggly cliffs they call home a few days after they're born.

Mountain goats wear built-in hiking boots—rough toe pads that help them grip.

PYGMY SEA HORSE

Little upright swimmers, sea horses live in shallow tropical and temperate waters throughout the world.

Unlike most fish, loyal sea horses pair up for life. The males carry the pair's eggs in a kangaroo-like pouch. When the babies (referred to as fry) hatch, they gallop out of the pouch in a wild herd of mini sea horses. The littlest species of sea horses are only half an inch (1.5 cm) tall; the largest can grow to be 14 inches (35 cm) tall.

This tiny fishy is also known as a dwarf puffer fish.

PEA PUFFER FISH

Don't scare that little pea puffer fish or he'll fill himself up with water like a loaded water balloon. His name is a true reflection of his adult size—he's really just the size of one little green pea pod—about an inch (2.5 cm) long. Found in the wild in India's Pamba River, these little cherubs have big appetites, eating loads of worms, snails, and shrimp.

MEERKAT

Native to parts of Africa, meerkats are constantly on alert for predators, such as jackals and falcons. Clever critters, meerkats share the group's work—including guard duty and babysitting. Everything is handled by working as a team. *Hakuna matata!* No worries!

Meerkats eat scorpions and snakes.

Meerkats peep, twitter, and bark.

BABY OCTOPUS

This little octopod hatchling squirms out of its shell as a small but complete version of its eight-legged parents. This helps the little ocean animal survive in superdark depths. But this little cephalopod is no shrinking violet. When it needs an escape, it shoots out tiny poofs of ink and sucks water into its gills, blasting water out of its funnel to jet away. And one more thing—that's no button nose. This baby sports a tiny beak!

A baby deep-sea octopus might have hundreds of siblings that hatch at the same time.

CHINCHILLA

Sweet, silvery chinchillas inhabit homes all over the world as pets, but in the wild, they are nearly extinct. Native to the Andes Mountains of South America, they come out of their rocky burrows at night to feed on plants. You might find it hard to believe that these silky soft little furballs are related to spiky, untouchable porcupines. Chinchillas look more like squirrels with cute little mouselike ears.

Chinchillas like to bathe in dust.

A fully grown male Galápagos sea lion can weigh up to 550 pounds (250 kg)!

SEA LION

Cool do! Sea lion pups are born with long hair called lanugo, which helps them keep warm until they develop blubber, or fat. Once this pup is a couple of months old, it can swim. By the time it's two years old, it can claim its reputation as one of the fastest mammals in the ocean, zipping through the water at bursts of up to 25 miles an hour (40 km/h).

LAMB

The wool from these adorable lambs is used to make carpets, but wool from other kinds of sheep is often used to make clothing. Depending on the breed, one sheep can produce enough wool each year for ten sweaters. They keep you warm *and* warm your heart!

A male lamb is sometimes called a "ram lamb."

GIANT PANDA

You *could* say a giant panda's stomach is a bottomless bamboo pit. Pandas chomp on bamboo plants up to 14 hours a day, moving only to search for more bamboo in China's forests. They've even developed a "false thumb"—an enlarged wrist bone that helps them grip the plants. All that eating doesn't leave much time for rest—they sleep for only 2 to 4 hours at a time.

Before they can walk, baby giant pandas build their muscles with stretches, kicks, wiggles, rolls, and crunches.

6 BEAUTIFUL

EASTERN COTTONTAIL
Even in captivity, a rescued wild cottontail will "wild up" at about three months old.

LOP-EARED
Social lop-eared rabbits (easily recognizable because of their floppy ears) come in many varieties, from the cashmere lop to the miniature lion lop to the American fuzzy.

ENGLISH ANGORA
These big balls of fur can actually be toilet trained, so they can run around the house without making a mess.

BUNNIES

FLEMISH GIANT
These docile rabbits can grow to be as big as a dog and love going for walks on a leash.

RESCUE BUNNY
Many animal shelters and rabbit rescue organizations have rescue bunnies for families willing to adopt.

LIONHEAD
This new domestic bunny breed may sport a woolly mane around its neck, but this bunny's personality is more like lapcat than lion.

Harvest mice weave round, grassy nests about the size of a baseball.

HARVEST MOUSE

With its teeny puffball body and its button nose, the harvest mouse is the smallest (and cutest) rodent in Britain. Its prehensile tail is often longer than its body and helps the mouse grip, hang from, and climb the tallest grass or twig. Sometimes young mice even link their tails together—like total BFFs.

GRAY WOLF

Puppy or predator? Gray wolves may grow up to hunt, but as pups they like to play. Young wolves have been seen tossing "toys" such as bones and animal skin to each other. As adults, they howl to "talk" to each other. Wolves live in close family units, helping take care of one another like humans do.

Wolves don't howl at the moon, but they do howl more during bright nights—when the moon is full.

MANATEE

These giant herbivores feed on a variety of plants, using their flippers to guide the food to their big bristly lips. Once in a while, a manatee might slurp up fish by accident.

These 1,200-pound (544-kg) gray swimmers are generally slow moving and love to eat grass—sea grass, that is! Early explorers may have mistaken these North American creatures for mermaids, but manatees are actually related to elephants. Unlike elephants, though, manatees have been known to bodysurf. They also like to meet up with their friends in areas where the water's warm.

Japanese macaques make snowballs!

Japanese macaque grandmothers have been observed helping raise their grandbabies.

JAPANESE MACAQUE

These pink-faced snow monkeys are found only in Japan. During the freezing winter, some groups treat themselves to a resort-style dip in natural hot springs. Others wash their food in salty seawater to give it a little extra flavor.

Tapirs are great swimmers and love to dive to nosh on aquatic plants.

TAPIR

For the first six months of its life, a tapir calf looks something like a furry watermelon with huge pinkish toes. In the wild, a baby tapir's stripes provide camouflage in the forest's dappled sunlight. This endangered species—found in Central and South America and Southeast Asia for tens of millions of years—is related to horses and rhinos.

A mother orangutan carries her baby until he learns to climb and swing by himself.

ORANGUTAN

This baby orangutan may have figured out the best part of life in the trees: just hanging out! Orangutans spend up to 95 percent of their time high up in trees on the Indonesian islands of Borneo and Sumatra. They sleep, eat, and play in nests that are big enough for a ten-year-old kid to stretch out in.

AMAZON GIANT GLASS FROG

Native to tropical Amazon forests, this frog's see-through skin helps it hide high in the trees. Sunlight shines right through the frog and provides camouflage. When it's time to lay its eggs, a glass frog deposits tiny white eggs onto a leaf above a stream. When the tadpoles emerge, they slip off the leaf and splash into the water below.

BEAVER

Busy beavers burrow into the banks of rivers and lakes, building dams to turn fields and forests into beloved ponds. They bring down trees and pack them with branches and mud to build cozy lodges. These big rodents live with their family and are herbivores that especially love the wood from willow trees.

Beavers sometimes build a lodge in the middle of a pond with concealed underwater entrances.

RESPLENDENT QUETZAL

Not counting its long tail feathers, this beauty is about the size of a pigeon.

Male resplendent quetzals have extravagant twin tail feathers that can grow to be three feet (1 m) long during the mating season. Once the eggs are in the nest, the male shares the work to keep the pair's light blue eggs warm. The only problem? That terrific tail isn't easy to tuck into the small hole in a tree where they live.

There are five different kinds of rhinos on Earth, but only the black rhino and white rhino live in Africa. Despite their names, both white and black rhinos are gray.

RHINOCEROS

A rhino's feelings wouldn't get hurt if you called it a name (not that you would). They have thick skin—literally. About an inch (2.5 cm) thick, rhino skin is built to protect the animal from thorns and biting flies. A rhino's size is nothing to mess with either. One of the world's biggest babies, rhinos can weigh 140 pounds (64 kg) at birth, gaining 4 pounds (2 kg) every day until they reach about 4,500 pounds (2,040 kg). Hugely adorable!

ROSE-RINGED PARAKEET

Noisy rose-ringed parakeets are native to Asia and Africa, but some that were once pets in the U.S. escaped and have set up wild colonies in Florida, Hawaii, and California.

HAMSTER

All hamsters today are related to one family of hamsters that lived in Syria around 1930.

GERBIL

Very social animals, gerbils greet each other by "kissing" each other's mouth or nose.

PETS

HEDGEHOG
The hedgehog got its name because of the way it grunts—like a little piggy—as it forages in the bushes.

GUINEA PIG
Guinea pigs jump up and down, or "popcorn," when they're happy.

TWO-TOED SLOTH

These shaggy tree dwellers sleep up to 20 hours a day and barely move at all even when they're awake. They're so sluggish, algae grows on their fur. Some scientists think their slow-moving ways help them hide from predators. The algae helps, too—the green hues blend right in with the trees the two-toed sloth hangs in.

When threatened by a predator, a two-toed sloth wakes up fast, biting, hissing, shrieking, and slashing with its claws.

SNOWY OWL

Unlike most owls, the snowy owl hunts at night and sometimes during the day. They're very patient, sitting on fence posts, barns, telephone poles—even roadside signs—watching and waiting. When their sharp senses tell them it's time, they jet off and snatch their prey (little lemmings are a favorite) with their sharp talons.

From their Arctic home, snowy owls migrate to Canada, the northern United States, Europe, and Asia.

A wolverine can smell a carcass buried under 20 feet (6 m) of snow.

WOLVERINE

So, what is a wolverine, anyway? It looks like a bear and its name sounds like a wolf relation. It's really a large weasel, weighing about 24 to 40 pounds (11 to 18 kg). It's very fierce, known to challenge real wolves over food and even take down large prey roughly 30 times its own size, like a 1,500-pound (680-kg) moose.

LION CUDDLES

THIS IS THE LIFE.

A lion can weigh up to 500 pounds (226 kg)—that's as much as a pony.

Lion cubs mimic their parents—running, stalking, and pouncing on their siblings and cousins for hours each day.

WITH MEERKAT

Pilanesberg, South Africa

Whenever Bob the meerkat got sleepy, he'd curl up in his favorite spot—between the paws of Zinzi the lion cub. "The animals would play in the morning and then cuddle together as they dozed," says San-Maré Pretorius, co-manager of Predator World, a zoo and game farm where the animals live. "They were inseparable."

The pair were introduced after their mothers abandoned them. Soon they were grooming each other, chasing one another, and snuggling when it was nap time. Zinzi liked to playfully leap at her meerkat buddy. Bob would run away but return a few seconds later to try to pounce on Zinzi! The mischievous meerkat would also sometimes snatch the cub's food or grasp on to her leg for a ride.

Zinzi moved back to the zoo's lion habitat when she was three months old. But the animals' friendship has had a long-lasting effect. Carefree Bob made Zinzi feel less nervous. And Bob had so much fun hanging with Zinzi, he's become friends with domestic cats that live at the zoo. Maybe these new pals will make good pillows, too!

Young lions probably can't wait to grow up. That's when they won't be the last ones to eat dinner, after the older males and females of the pride get theirs. Adult females do most of the hunting, while males patrol and defend their territory.

BUMBLEBEE BAT

One of the world's smallest mammals, this cave-dwelling bat is also called the Kitti's hog-nosed bat. It lives in caves in Southeast Asia and loves to eat insects. The bitty bumblebee bat weighs less than one-tenth of an ounce (2 g)—that's less than the weight of one dime—and is only about one inch (2.5 cm) long. Although its tail is so small you might not believe it's there, the bat's snout nose is hard to miss.

Everything about the bumblebee bat is small, except its relatively huge ears.

PYGMY HIPPO

At six feet (2 m) long and weighing as much as 600 pounds (272 kg), this bristly lipped pygmy is no pip-squeak. Pygmy hippos hide out along the riverbanks of West Africa by day and come out of the water at night to eat fallen fruit, grass, and leaves. Built like submarines, a pygmy hippo's eyes, ears, and nose sit at the top of its head so it can see, hear, and smell while the rest of its body is submerged. Its ears and nose shut tight when it dives underwater.

The pygmy hippo is about one-tenth the size of a common hippo.

CAPYBARA

Although it's a close relation of the guinea pig, the capybara will grow to be much too big for your pocket pet's cage. He prefers the aquatic lifestyle. In the wild, the barrel-shaped rodent can be found along the grassy banks of rivers, streams, and ponds of South America. A capybara can swim as well as he can walk. He can stay underwater for up to five minutes if he needs to hide from a hungry predator, like a jaguar or a huge anaconda.

The capybara's scientific name, *Hydrochoerus*, means "water hog."

Related to raccoons and kinkajous, these two-pound (1-kg) cuties live in foggy mountain forests in Ecuador and Colombia.

Four subspecies of olinguitos exist, each with their own size and color— variations of orange, red, and brown.

COVERED

...ga Nature Reserve, Ecuador

...all of fuzz has caused quite a buzz. Until recently, no one knew that the mammal now ... the olinguito (oh-lin-GHEE-toh) existed—though some had been living in plain sight. ...ocals in parts of South America had seen them in forests, and one had even lived ...oo," says John Gibbons of the Smithsonian Institution, which revealed the animal's ...very in 2013. "We thought they belonged to another, similar-looking species." Biologist ...ofer Helgen found hints of the olinguito's existence about ten years ago while ...ying bones at a museum. "Looking closely, he realized that they didn't look like any ...n creature," Gibbons says. DNA tests showed that the animal was a new species. ...his is the first new carnivore discovered in the Americas in 35 years," biologist Roland ... says. To spot living olinguitos, Kays, Helgen, and other scientists trekked to fog-filled ...ntain forests in Ecuador, where the museum bones were found. There, they spotted ...eral olinguitos lounging in trees and chomping figs. ...low scientists want to closely study olinguitos, since not too much is known about ...m. "We do know that they're amazing," Gibbons says. "And they prove that there's more ...uncover in our world."

WHERE'S MY WELCOME PARTY?

There are four species of dik-dik, each with a different shaped nose.

DIK-DIK

One of the smallest of the ungulates (animals with toed hooves, like buffalo, deer, and goats), the rare and dainty dik-dik is a tiny antelope that lives in Africa. These animals live in areas with dense cover, where they can find plenty of food, keep cool in the shade, and hide from predators such as lions, leopards, cheetahs, and pythons.

The
tamandua
has a prehensile
tail that acts as a
third arm, grabbing
tree limbs for
support.

TAMANDUA

The timid tamandua may look like a super-cuddly little anteater, but if you make it mad, watch out. With a mouth smaller than a lima bean, it can't bite. But it might hiss, spray you with a very unpleasant odor, screech, and threaten you with sharp claws.

HIDDEN GEMS

The Latin word *lemures* means "ghost."

PYGMY MOUSE LEMUR

The large-eyed pygmy mouse lemur from Madagascar could fit in a teacup. At 2.25 to 4.75 inches (6 to 12 cm) tall, it's the smallest primate in the world. Active mostly at night, this tree dweller comes out to snack on insects, fruit, and flowers.

Quokkas can climb trees.

QUOKKA

The quokka of Western Australia is a relative of the kangaroo and most closely resembles its cousin, the wallaby. This marvel of the outback lives in small family groups that work together to create tunnels through the underbrush. The tunnels make it easier to find food, and also provide getaway routes if they have to hop away from a predator.

CUSCUS

A relative of the opossum, the secretive cuscus spends its life in the trees—swinging from branch to branch with help from its prehensile tail. This Australian cuddler sleeps during the day and searches for food at night. It eats leaves and fruit and, on special occasions, small birds and tasty reptiles.

Scientists originally believed the cuscus was a monkey.

DWARF FLYING SQUIRREL

It's a bird! It's a plane! It's a ... super-squeaky flying rodent? The Japanese dwarf flying squirrel lives in the forests of Japan. With an elastic membrane between its forelegs and hind legs stretched out like a cape, this tiny aviator glides from tree to tree. He's looking for seeds, fruit, and leaves to eat. With its belly full by morning, this nocturnal nugget tucks into a hole in a tree to rest for the day.

A Japanese dwarf flying squirrel makes its nest (called a drey) out of sticks and leaves.

When threatened, lesser mouse deer stomp like crazy to scare off predators.

LESSER MOUSE DEER

Is it a mouse that looks like a deer, or a deer that looks like a mouse? The lesser mouse deer looks like a little of both, but it is actually from an animal family that includes hippos, deer, and pigs. This shy little deer doesn't have antlers or horns, but males do sport tusklike teeth.

COW

This calf may help its buddies take over the world! There are about 1.5 billion cows on Earth—that's nearly five times as many cows as there are people in the United States. In fact, cows outnumber people in nine U.S. states, including Oklahoma and Idaho.

A young calf will grow into a cow that chews about 50 times a minute.

BABY EMPEROR PENGUIN

As soon as a baby emperor is safe and warm under Dad's feathers, Mom leaves it to go find food. Soon enough she returns with a mouthful of food for the youngster.

The largest of all penguins, emperor penguins "porpoise," or poke their heads above water to breathe.

GOLDEN LION TAMARIN

Golden lion tamarins may look like a tiny version of the lion, but don't let those thick manes fool you—these smart little primates are all about the monkey business. Living in the trees of Brazil's Atlantic coastal rain forests, they live in social groups, carry their young on their backs, and travel from branch to branch looking for a meal. Their favorite finger foods? Insects, fruit, lizards, and small bird eggs.

CLOWNFISH

Before a clownfish settles down with the poisonous anemone where it lives, the fish softly touches the anemone's tentacles. This little dance helps the striped fish acclimate to its reef home. A slimy substance on the fish protects it from the host's poison. Once the fish is settled, it helps its host keep clean. In return, the anemone protects the small fish from bigger, hungry fish.

An anemone is actually a reef animal that looks like a plant.

OTTER ADORES

Somerset, England

After Otto the otter finished his daily bathtub swim, he'd dry off. But not with a towel. The cub would rub his soggy head against his four kitten friends. "The kitties loved Otto," says Pauline Kidner, founder of the Secret World Wildlife Center where the otter lives. "They even let him use them as hair dryers!"

Otto arrived at Secret World after he was found abandoned on a riverbank. To keep him from getting lonely, caretakers introduced the otter to a litter of newborn kittens. At first the babies mostly slept. "They would snuggle real close and wrap their limbs around each other for warmth," Kidner says. As they grew, they became inseparable playmates. One favorite toy was Otto's tail, which the kittens batted with their paws. Otto liked to playfully chase the cats as they bounded around their home.

Soon the kittens were adopted, and now Otto is bonding with another otter at the center. Luckily Otto's new buddy—like his kitty pals—doesn't mind getting a little wet.

STOP HOGGING THE OTTER.

KITTEN PALS

Not much beats being rocked to sleep in the water. When this critter was a baby, it spent most of its time on its mother's belly while she floated around. Otters are built for aquatic life. They have water-repellent fur, webbed back feet, and nostrils and ears that close when they're underwater.

While river otters swim on their bellies, slippery sea otters prefer the backstroke.

6 COLD-BLOODED

BOX TURTLE
Thanks to its hinged design, a box turtle's shell slams shut when it's threatened. This tough defensive mechanism also has the ability to regenerate itself if damaged.

GREEN IGUANA
A green iguana can grow to be as long as an NBA basketball player is tall.

AXOLOTL
This cute little salamander with pink feathery gills can be found in Mexico. These critters can live for 15 years, surviving on tasty treats like worms and shellfish.

CUTIES

LEOPARD GECKO
The gentle leopard gecko is famous not only for its spots but also for its urine, which comes out as tiny crystals.

CHAMELEON
The chameleon is famous for being able to change its color, but did you know its tongue can be longer than its body?

CORN SNAKE
Colorful corn snakes can grow to about five feet (1.5 m) long and have beautiful patterns of brown, red, and orange.

AMERICAN PIKA

As a baby, the American pika is only about as big as a walnut. Adults are about as big as a baseball. The American pika looks like a big mouse but is more closely related to the rabbit. It spends much of its time eating, nibbling on plants, and storing food for winter in piles called haystacks.

With thick fur and round bodies to conserve heat, American pikas excel at staying warm in cold climates.

I am pika, hear me roar!

A group of foxes is called a skulk.

ARCTIC FOX

An arctic fox's white coat may be beautiful, but it serves a purpose: keeping the fox warm in über-cold temperatures as low as minus 58°F (-50°C). It also disguises the fox in the snow and ice, protecting it from hungry predators, such as polar bears, wolves, and raptors. In spring, its coat changes from white to brown or gray to blend in with exposed rocks on the spring tundra.

The slender loris uses its toes to hang upside down from a branch so it can grab food.

SLENDER LORIS

A baby slender loris grips its mother's fur with tiny fingers and peeks out at the world with huge eyes. In India, the tears of the slender loris are thought to have medicinal properties. As a result of this belief, poachers will capture these wild primates from their natural habitat to harvest their tears and sometimes even sell the animals into the exotic pet trade.

CHIMPANZEE

This little ape might be having fun, but there are brains behind its party attitude. Chimps, which live in the tropical forests of Africa, are extremely intelligent. They use sticks as tools to "fish" for bugs in logs, and crush leaves in their mouths to soak up drinking water like sponges.

Chimpanzees are like human kids—if they find something fun, they'll hoot, holler, and scream until their friends come check it out.

COMMON LOON

Bird on board! When feathery loon chicks hatch they're almost immediately on the go—Mom carries her little ones on her back to protect them from predators. By the time the young loons of North America grow up, they can dive down nearly 250 feet (76 m) and hold their breath for up to eight minutes as they fish.

Loons are named for the clumsy way they walk on land.

JAPANESE EMPEROR CATERPILLAR

This little green crawler is destined for greatness as the larva of the great Japanese emperor butterfly, the national butterfly of Japan. Before their glorious transformations, you might see them munching on hackberries in preparation. They may seem tiny and sluggish as youngsters, but soon they'll gracefully take flight. You can find them in their native Japan, on the Korean Peninsula, or in China, Taiwan, and Vietnam.

Donkeys make excellent guard animals, sometimes protecting herds of cattle, goats, or sheep.

DONKEY

This type of miniature donkey once lived in wild herds on the Italian islands of Sicily and Sardinia. Today, they are often found as barnyard pets.

BABY CHEETAH

Tampa Bay, Florida, U.S.A.

Whenever Kasi the cheetah wants Mtani the Labrador retriever's attention, he chirps like a baby bird. Mtani responds by chasing Kasi's tail. "They absolutely love spending time together," says zoologist Mike Boos of Busch Gardens Tampa Bay, where the friends live.

The animals were introduced shortly after Kasi was abandoned by his mother. The baby cheetah was sad and alone, so caretakers found him a pal. They brought Mtani from an animal shelter and began supervising playdates for the pair.

Now Kasi and Mtani spend most of their days cuddling, rolling around in the grass of the park's cheetah habitat, and playing tug-of-war with stuffed animal toys. They even share a large pillow when they snooze, with Kasi often falling asleep right on top of Mtani! If the cheetah is separated from his Lab friend, he chirps until the dog returns. Luckily, the buddies have a lot of together time in their future: They've started traveling the country with their keepers, helping teach people about endangered animals such as cheetahs. Says Boos, "The two will be friends for life."

A LITTLE LESS SLOBBER, PLEASE!

Under the shield of tall African grass, cheetah cubs hide from hungry lions and hyenas. The cubs' long, fuzzy coats, called mantles, camouflage them from danger. As they grow, the mantles recede, but they'll keep their manes until they're about two years old.

GETS PET DOG

In Africa, farmers use livestock guardian dogs like Anatolian shepherds to protect livestock against predators like cheetahs.

Cheetahs make facial expressions that signal what kind of mood they're in.

BAT-EARED FOX

The bat-eared fox is in the same family of animals as wolves, coyotes, and even your family dog.

This little fox's oversize ears help him hunt by tuning in to the tiny noises made by the lizards and bugs that it loves to eat. Those ears (they stretch to five inches/12.5 cm tall) also help bat-eared foxes protect themselves from predators like cheetahs, hyenas, and pythons. When a bat-eared fox hears a predator coming, it streaks off in a zigzag pattern to escape.

Scientists disagree on whether the red panda is related to the giant panda, the raccoon, or another family.

RED PANDA

Bamboo, *delish!* These "fire foxes," as they're sometimes called, dine on bamboo just as their black-and-white namesake does. But unlike giant pandas, Asia's red pandas have cute white whiskers. The sensitive hairs help the pandas navigate narrow spaces, especially at night.

KANGAROO

Talk about tough! Thanks to their huge feet and strong hind legs, kangaroos can hop 25 feet (7.5 m) in a single bound, jump up three times their height, and travel 35 miles an hour (56 km/h). Kangaroos live in eastern Australia in troops or herds. They're marsupials, which means a kangaroo mom carries her baby (called a joey) in a built-in pouch.

WALRUS

Who's a good walrus? This big baby walrus might look like it needs a shave, but when it grows up, those bristly whiskers will help it detect food, like shellfish, from under the ocean bottom. Once the prey is found, an adult walrus will dig it out. If that doesn't work, it might drill for the shellfish by squirting water with its tongue. Then the walrus sucks out the shellfish meat in one supersize slurp.

The walrus' scientific name *(Odobenus rosmarus)* means "tooth-walking sea horse."

A walrus might use his tusks (which can grow to three feet/1 m) to haul itself out of the water or to break a breathing hole through the ice from below.

PORCUPINE

Baby porcupines may look cuddly, but they'll soon have the ultimate defense—quills! The soft, bendable quills that make this youngster look almost huggable quickly harden in a few days. As many as 30,000 sharp, barbed quills protect this living pincushion from any hungry predators.

A porcupine can use its tail like an extra leg to prop up its rear end.

SERVAL

People sometimes refer to the serval as the "giraffe cat" because of its long neck. But this cat is no herbivore. It's a serious predator—maybe even the most successful hunter of all cats. It tracks small mammals underground and can leap up to catch a bird in flight, slamming its front paws together in a knockout that stuns its prey before it delivers a fatal bite to the prey's neck. We wouldn't want to get on this cat's bad side!

A serval can have spots and stripes.

MARMOSET

When they're chatting with fellow marmosets, these mannerly monkeys wait their turn to talk. Scientists study conversations between these extremely social and talkative primates to better understand the roots of human conversation. From Brazil, these mini-monkeys stand about seven inches (18 cm) tall and live about 12 years in their wild forest homes.

Little marmosets use their big teeth to gnaw holes in trees and get sap.

101

The raccoon has an excellent sense of touch and uses its front paws like little hands.

I'M NOT SURE WHICH RACCOON THIS IS. THE MASK HIDES HIS IDENTITY.

A hungry raccoon will happily jump into the water to catch a fish.

ADOPTS CAT

Warstein, Germany

Raccoons often hang out with their mom and siblings, so it'd be pretty unusual for one to invite a *cat* to a family gathering. But that's exactly what this raccoon seems to have done. The cat cuddles with the raccoon and its family as they lounge on rocks, and snoozes with them in a cave. The masked gang even lets the kitty have first dibs when feeding time rolls around.

Most cats are solitary, and raccoons can be territorial. So rangers at Wildpark Warstein tried to remove the cat several times. But the feline always returned to the welcoming paws of the raccoon family. "Raccoons often live in families," park chief Henning Dictus says. "I think the raccoons see the cat as part of theirs." Just don't mess with this cat's new fam: If humans get too close to his adopted gang, he'll jump out in front with a protective but friendly "meow."

This young raccoon might be an expert climber—many raccoons spend their first few months living in a nest in a tree hole. As adults, raccoons rely more on their sense of touch than their senses of sight and smell to find meals such as frogs, bird eggs, insects, and even snakes.

SUGAR GLIDER

These pink-nosed mini-marsupials love sweets, like sap from eucalyptus trees, flower blossoms, pollen, nectar, and bugs. At night, they stretch open their winglike membranes, called patagium, to slice through the air, gliding from branch to branch in search of food. Life is so grand in the trees, they rarely touch the ground.

EGYPTIAN TORTOISE

The Egyptian tortoise, also known as Kleinmann's tortoise or Leith's tortoise, is one of the teeniest tortoises of all. Males make a mating call that sounds like a birdcall. When a female is ready to lay her little eggs, she digs a burrow and a few months later, a small clutch of coin-size tortoises use little claws to crack their way out.

Egyptian tortoises are a critically endangered species.

Male sugar gliders have a bald spot on their heads that is actually a scent gland.

Ermines are usually found on the ground, but they like to climb trees and swim, too.

ERMINE

Hares, beware! This critter could be your enemy. Silent and sneaky, the one-foot (30.5-cm)-long ermine can pounce on prey that's larger than it is, such as an arctic hare. The stealthy stalker gets help from its changing coat, which is white during winter and brown in spring and summer—perfect for blending in with its surroundings.

FAREWELL

As adults, rosy maple moths don't feed at all. They retain all of their energy from what they ate as small caterpillars. That's why, when they're hatched from their eggs, they are very hungry caterpillars!

Index

Index

110

Credits

Staff for This Book

Ariane Szu-Tu, *Project Editor*
Julide Dengel, *Art Director*
Kelley Miller, *Senior Photo Editor*
Ruth Ann Thompson, *Designer*
Paige Towler, *Editorial Assistant*
Michelle Harris, *Researcher*
Sanjida Rashid, *Design Production Assistant*
Erica Holsclaw, *Special Projects Assistant*
Michael Cassady, *Rights Clearance Specialist*
Grace Hill, *Managing Editor*
Joan Gossett, *Senior Production Editor*
Lewis R. Bassford, *Production Manager*
Darrick McRae, *Manager, Production Services*
Rahsaan Jackson, *Imaging*
Susan Borke, *Legal and Business Affairs*

Contributing Writers: Kitson Jazynka, John Micklos, Jr., Kate Olesin, Jen Rini, B. F. Summers, C. M. Tomlin, Sarah Youngson

Based on the "Cute Animals" feature series and the "Incredible Animal Friends" and "Amazing Animals" departments in *National Geographic Kids* **magazine**

Rachel Buchholz, *Editor and Vice President*
Catherine D. Hughes, *Senior Science Editor*
Andrea Silen, Kay Boatner, *Associate Editors*
Kelley Miller, *Senior Photo Editor;* Lisa Jewell, *Photo Editor*
Eileen O'Tousa-Crowson, *Art Director;* Julide Dengel, *Designer;* Stephanie Rudig, *Associate Digital Designer*
Nick Spagnoli, *Copy Editor*
Rose Davidson, *Special Projects Assistant*

Published by the National Geographic Society

Gary E. Knell, *President and CEO*
John M. Fahey, *Chairman of the Board*
Melina Gerosa Bellows, *Chief Education Officer*
Declan Moore, *Chief Media Officer*
Hector Sierra, *Senior Vice President and General Manager, Book Division*

Senior Management Team, Kids Publishing and Media

Nancy Laties Feresten, *Senior Vice President;* Jennifer Emmett, *Vice President, Editorial Director, Kids Books;* Julie Vosburgh Agnone, *Vice President, Editorial Operations;* Rachel Buchholz, *Editor and Vice President,* NG Kids *magazine;* Michelle Sullivan, *Vice President, Kids Digital;* Eva Absher-Schantz, *Design Director;* Jay Sumner, *Photo Director;* Hannah August, *Marketing Director;* R. Gary Colbert, *Production Director*

Digital

Anne McCormack, *Director;* Laura Goertzel, Sara Zeglin, *Producers;* Jed Winer, *Special Projects Assistant;* Emma Rigney, *Creative Producer;* Brian Ford, *Video Producer;* Bianca Bowman, *Assistant Producer;* Natalie Jones, *Senior Product Manager*

The National Geographic Society is one of the world's largest nonprofit scientific and educational organizations. Founded in 1888 to "increase and diffuse geographic knowledge," the Society's mission is to inspire people to care about the planet. It reaches more than 400 million people worldwide each month through its official journal, *National Geographic,* and other magazines; National Geographic Channel; television documentaries; music; radio; films; books; DVDs; maps; exhibitions; live events; school publishing programs; interactive media; and merchandise. National Geographic has funded more than 10,000 scientific research, conservation, and exploration projects and supports an education program promoting geographic literacy.

For more information, please visit nationalgeographic.com, call 1-800-NGS LINE (647-5463), or write to the following address:
National Geographic Society
1145 17th Street N.W.
Washington, D.C. 20036-4688 U.S.A.

Visit us online at nationalgeographic.com/books

For librarians and teachers: ngchildrensbooks.org

More for kids from National Geographic:
kids.nationalgeographic.com

For information about special discounts for bulk purchases, please contact National Geographic Books Special Sales: ngspecsales@ngs.org

For rights or permissions inquiries, please contact National Geographic Books Subsidiary Rights: ngbookrights@ngs.org

Paperback ISBN: 978-1-4263-1887-0
Reinforced library binding ISBN: 978-1-4263-1888-7

Printed in the United States of America
15/CK-CML/1